KID'S PASSOVER Activity Book

ILLUSTRATED BY
DEVORA KIM

LANG
BOOK PUBLISHING

LANG
BOOK PUBLISHING

langbookpublishing.com

No part of this book may be reproduced, stored in a retrieval system, or transmitted by any means, electronic, mechanical, photocopying, recording, or otherwise without written permission from the author.

Copyright © Devora Kim 2017. All rights reserved.

The right of Devora Kim to be identified as author of the Work has been asserted by her in accordance with the New Zealand Copyright Act 1994.

National Library of New Zealand Cataloguing-in-Publication Data
Lang Book Publishing 2017

Illustrations by Devora Kim

ISBN 978-0-9941422-1-4 – Paperback

Published in New Zealand
A catalogue record for this book is available from the National Library of New Zealand.
Kei te pātengi raraunga o Te Puna Mātauranga o Aotearoa te whakarārangi o tēnei pukapuka.

Lighting the Holiday Candles

Karpas

Appetizer

Separating the Afikomen

Mah Nishtanah
The Four Questions

The Youngest Child

The First Plague

Blood

The Second Plague

The Third Plague

Lice

The Fourth Plague

Arov Noxious Creatures

The Fifth Plague
The Livestock Disease

The Sixth Plague

The Seventh Plague
Hail

The Eighth Plague

Locusts

The Ninth Plague

Darkness

The Tenth Plague

The Death of the First Born

The Seder Plate

Rachtzah
Handwashing

Matzah
Blessing

Maror
Bitter Herb

Finding and Eating the Afikomen

The Third Cup
*** The Cup of Redemption***

Four Cups of Wine

See you in Jerusalem

www.ingramcontent.com/pod-product-compliance
Lightning Source LLC
LaVergne TN
LVHW070951070426
835507LV00031B/3493